My Mother Told Me!
Why Didn't Your Mother Tell You?
by Machina Ervin

© Copyright 2007

Paperback edition of this book published by: Big Erv Publishing 2008

My Mother Told Me! Why Didn't Your Mother Tell You? Copyright© 2004.
No part of this book may be used or reproduced in any way without written permission from the author.

This book can be purchased from BigErvPublishing.com or write
Big Erv Publishing, 91 Boerum Street, Brooklyn, NY 11206.

Cover Concept: Machina Ervin
Cover Work: Jason Harrison
Typset work: Jason Harrison (www.jayharry.com)

Library Of Congress has cataloged this text as follows:
Library of Congress Control Number: 2008909202
Papeback Edition.

Ervin, Machina
My Mother Told Me! Why Didn't Your Mother Tell You?
ISBN 978-0-9814514-0-4

Disclaimer: This book is based on my life and my opinion's. I may have experienced some things and some things I have heard in passing but this book is in no way to down grade men or women. I am not a professional therapist or psychologist, so for those who read this book it is no different than someone else who writes a book based on their life. This book is based solely on what my mother told me, not to show up other mothers or women period. You live your life how you feel you want to live it I just hope I can help in some small way.

Introduction

I wrote this book to help all people who think they don't have choices. This book is written to educate, warn you and challenge your current mode of thinking. This book is a tool to help you be who you really are and the person your parents raised you to be. As we go through our lives we always want to play the blame game. Well stop blaming everyone else, break the cycle and change! A line from the song always stuck with me. It said, "If you want to be someone else just, change your mind". So as you read this book, make up your mind that by the end of this book you can change.

My mother gave me very solid advice all of my life and I want to share it with the world. The older I become the more I realize that most parents didn't do the same for their children and that may be why most adults make so many unnecessary mistakes. I am not saying that parents are all knowing and all seeing. Most are so busy providing the basics that giving their children good solid advice just goes by the wayside.

I want you to think of this book as a place to turn to when the outside world is pushing in on you. So enjoy. You can change!

Dedication

I dedicate this book to my mom without whom this book wouldn't even be possible. She not only sacrificed so much to raise me, but she also gave to me when I didn't deserve it and loved me when I wasn't easy to love. So all I have to say is: Mom, it is now your turn to live and enjoy!

I LOVE YOU!

Acknowledgments

I would to acknowledge my proofer and editor Grace Fulop without her this really would not be a possible. She was helpful and very fair.

Thank you Grace.

I'd love to thank my dear friend Jason. Truly and honestly this book would not have gotten off the ground without you. You are the world's best graphics man! Big Jay!

My Mother Told Me! Why Didn't Your Mother Tell You?

Chapters

1. Life
2. Women
3. Men
4. Money
5. Education
6. Careers
7. Children
8. Love
9. Friends
10. Family
11. Marriage

My Mother Told Me! Why Didn't Your Mother Tell You?

CHAPTER 1

LIFE

Face Your Fears!

Life is full of ups and downs, but it is up to you to decide that life is not going to beat you up! I find that most people go through their whole lives just avoiding things. What I mean is, most people avoid their fears instead of facing them and overcoming them.

I was in a relationship with someone and he left me because he feared being hurt. When he made that decision, he didn't count on me saying, "I don't want to be friends". He planned for me to live his by his fear, No! No! No! I felt sorry for him because, instead of, facing the fears. He let the fears conquer him and he lost a good relationship.

I tried to help him see that he needed to change his behavior and better his own life. He never wanted to go forward with anything for fear of the unknown. So, he decided to stay in the same situation with friends who are going nowhere, just settling for a job, not a career.

I learned a valuable lesson from him: make better choices!

Be a Leader Not a Follower!

We hear this term a lot, but do we really get it? My mother always told me that each person who you see on drugs someone turned them on to it.

Every drug user had that one encounter with someone who said to try this and, for whatever reason, the person tried it and liked it!

I had a friend who was very rebellious. When I met her, I thought hey she would be my friend. Until I saw her for who she really was. I was never the type to disobey my mom until I met her. As my mother puts it, I met people who urged me to exert my independence. But it cost me.

So, always lead your own parade, never be a band member. Don't get me wrong. Support others because you want others to support you. Just make sure that it is the right parade.

All Relationships are Work.

People don't realize that every person in their lives represents a relationship. As we go through life, we think that only our romances are our relationships. In fact that is untrue. We are in a relationship with everyone we decide to get close to.

I heard someone say that 60% of life is just work. So, that works out like this: our love lives, our children and our personal fun are work. We have to make adjustments all the time. Realizing that relationships are a form of work will help us adjust better.

Be Willing To Admit your Faults and When You're Wrong.

Most people have a problem admitting when they are wrong. Most people never admit their faults, their rebellion, pride and immaturity cause them to lose good people. If you just say, "I was wrong". The other person will respect and maybe even love you. Taking this action will cut through all the nonsense. Most people like drama: if you put a stop to the drama before it begins, it can't grow.

I find that most people have a problem with pride. Pride can cause you to not only have not only messed up personal relationships, but professional ones too!

Yes, if you can be the bigger person, you will be the more mature person. You will be the bigger person and have a healthier life.

You Don't Have to Lose Your Temper To Get Your Point Across.

When you are talking to people and they get you really angry, you have a choice you can blurt something out or just stop. Take the time and think it through and say to ask your self, "Am I going to let this person get to me like this"? No one is worth losing who you are.

You can stop and think how this going to affect you in the long run. And as for temper, you can just get rid of it. Just take a time out for your self.

Don't Be A Doormat.

We all have these moments when we say, "Why did I let this happen"? We usually answer ourselves with a lot of excuses, but we never question ourselves further. "Why I do this over and over again" and "What am I getting out of letting people walk all over me"? Most people who allow themselves to be treated as doormats usually get some kind of gratification in return. My mother and I always look at those people are and say they're into a Sadomasochistic behavior.

I've especially seen women be a doormat for men over and over again. The men would just treat them horribly. The funny thing is, they never left the men. I always wondered why they would stay after that kind of treatment. The answer is, they don't value themselves. Don't be a doormat.

Avoid The Crowd!

As a child, I always used to hear my grandmother say, "It is better to say 'There she goes' than 'there she lay.'" As I got older I got it! She was saying, when you see things break out, take a look around, stop, think and run in the opposite direction.

This is true in the case of my mother. My mom worked in downtown Manhattan, not too far from the World Trade Center. On September 11, 2001*, my mom was waiting for the minivan to take her from 388 Greenwich Street to the World Trade Center. The van was taking too long, she jumped on the train. Well, she decided not to get off the train at the Trade Center stop go on to the doctor office, which is 4 blocks away from the Trade Center. She is in the room getting her therapy and her doctor comes in and says "Ruth, a plane just hit the Trade Center." My mom says to him, "Who told you that?" "He says the receptionist just told me." My mom said, "I don't believe you because they didn't hear anything." She tells him, "Don't you have a laptop? Go and check." All of a sudden she hears a big bang, the building shakes, the machine she was using starts blinking, the doctor runs in the room and says "It's true, it's true. "A plane hit the Trade Center." "My mom says, we're outta here!"

My mother leaves gets down stairs, there are lots of people standing around on the streets smoking and talking, no one is moving and there is debris falling from the sky. My mother says this is incredible. She goes down into the train station and asks the token booth clerk if the train is still running; the token booth clerk says, "yes." She gets on the train. There is hardly anyone on the train and she is shocked. My mother said she was home watching on television when the buildings fell and watched as the crowds walked over the bridges.

One week later, one of our doctors called us just to see if we were okay. My mother said, "Yes, I am fine." He begins to tell my mother about how he got stuck in Manhattan until 6:30 pm. My mother gets off the phone and says, "If they had all left with me, they could have been with me in comfort and out of the way of danger, but they followed the crowd."

So avoid the crowd in all ways!

*On this day I lost many of my old co-workers in the World Trade Center tragedy, I too have a story and was affected, so to all of those friends and family members who lost someone my prayers and thoughts are with you today and always.

Reconcile Your Past.

When I look at us human beings, I see a bunch of messed up people. People go through life never dealing with the issues of the past. People are walking dead. Meaning they walk around in a fog, most of the time.

I dated a man whose mother died when he was a child and he never got over her death. I, along with several other people, used to tell him that he should talk to someone about it. He said he could handle it. I was the one who forced him to deal with that issue and now he thanks me. I have known several people who have had childhood trauma and they are trying to have that childhood they missed as adults. You can't make up for lost time or for things you didn't have.

You need to accept that whatever happened, happened, and say that you will get over it and move on.

Don't Help Those Who don't Want To Be Helped.

I learned a long, long time ago that if someone doesn't ask you for help, most of the time they don't want your help. People are always asking people for help in some form or fashion, but the kicker is that people really don't want help.

When I go through life, I look at people and say, "Why didn't you just ask me?" I knew someone who had a cousin who was having baby. They were running around trying to find a hall where they could hold the baby shower. At no time did my friend ask me of a place. Then after all of the failed attempts and promises not kept, he finally turned to me and I gave him some information and the baby shower went off without a hitch.

The lesson there is he didn't ask me until he became desperate. When you give out unasked advice, all you are asking for is rejection. Also, you are casting your pearls among swine. Information is to be shared but only with those who want it, not those who are not going to do anything with it or those who are going to abuse it.

Knowledge is too valuable just to hand out like a piece of candy it is to be cherished.

To Whom Much is Given Much is Required!

In life we all want more, but more is not always good. I hear people say all the time, "If I had a lot of money, I would do this," or "If I was given more responsible position, I would do this." Number one, you don't know what you would do until you are put into that position and, furthermore, more financial responsibility doesn't mean that you will be more financially literate.

People have this dream that if only they were given a chance, they would show the world. Maybe the reason they were not given the chance is because they may not be ready…if given the chance most of us would fail. Why? Simple. The human motive is: FEAR and SELF PROTECTION. Most people would become greedy or power hungry.

Have you ever heard the saying, "MANY ARE CALLED, BUT FEW ARE CHOSEN"? Each person on this planet is called to do something. Your job is to find out what that is!

So, the thought I leave you with is, don't ask for something because you just might get it!" Are you prepared?

Be Comfortable With Being Different!

People who go around with different color hair or who dress weird, are trying to be accepted. They may say, "No, I am just expressing myself," but if they were accepted, they wouldn't be doing that.

When kids go to school and they think different than the rest of the kids, they feel rejected. Then they start dressing weird and having these weird hairdos'. If kids accepted them, they wouldn't do that. Now more than at any other time, children are subject to peer pressure and bullying. Children who are made fun of now resort to killing other kids who reject them. If those children's parents had told them to just be comfortable with being different, it wouldn't matter if kids accepted them or not.

Now that I am an adult, I find that I have been different all of my life. Meaning, I have always been smart and physically fit. I have finally come to accept that. When I was a child, I was ridiculed for it, also so what I did was lower my standards to fit in with the crowd. That never gets you anywhere but down the tubes.

Even women with men don't put up with the mess that men usually cause. Just for that you are different. Don't settle.

Be comfortable with being different!

Learn To Be A Lover Of Truth and Freedom!

In my 33 years of living I have always been a lover of truth and freedom, but I find that most people are not. I try to get people to see the truth, but they don't want to. As my mother says, "People don't want the truth they like their bondage." Every time I hear that, it blows my mind. I think to myself, "Why are people so hung up on games, lies and deceit?"

I've come to a couple of conclusions: People only do what they know and they only do what doesn't cause them any pain. Truth is about pain and so is freedom because, to be free, you will have to endure some kind of temporary pain. As people should know by reading about slavery in America, the slaves endured years of bondage. For them to one day wake up and say, "I want my freedom," was a deep thing. People were leaving a life where everything was provided for them, even if it wasn't the best. Freedom always costs you something. The question is: Are you willing to pay the cost?

Truth has a price tag, too, but you are willing to give up things once you know the truth. I'm sure you have seen The Matrix, starring Keanu Reeves. The whole picture was about him finding out the truth and, once he found out the truth, could he accept it and not want to go back to being deceived. That is the problem with most of us once we are faced with the truth it is too hard to accept and we want to go back to being in the dark. Because the truth you see is never pretty, whether it is about us or about other people.

When you don't love truth or freedom you lose. You live a life of not seeing things for what they really are. But if you choose to not want freedom and truth, that is your choice, too!

Make Better Choices.

Oh! This is one thing that really gets me. I have heard people say, "I know that I shouldn't do this and I know it is going to cost me but I'm going to do this anyway."

I dated a guy who broke up with me because he was having a difficult time at the time. I told him, "You are leaving me because you can't deal with having a relationship, and problems, too." He said, "yes." I asked him "Do you realize the choice you are making?" He said I know this might be the biggest mistake of my life, but if it is one, let me make it." I said, "I understand but I don't agree." He could not accept that. I thought to myself that he would be calling me in a couple of months. Sure enough, he called five months later apologizing, saying he was sorry he left me and the decision was not a good one. I tried to tell him five months before. When he came back, he wanted us to resume the relationship and I said, "No, that is my choice. I love me too much to be subject to all of your bad choices."

My thought that I am trying to convey is that choices are what make our lives go round and they could go around much smoother if we made better choices.

You Can't Do What You Don't Know.

In this life we always ask people why they didn't you do this or that. People cannot do what they don't know. We put too much pressure on people when they make bad decisions or when they don't do what we think they should do.

My mother and I talk about this all the time and we come to the conclusion that some people are not rebellious or stubborn, they just don't know another way. The bigger question is: If they did know another way, would they make a better choice?

All of us sometimes make choices that we regret, but, if we were better informed, would we make the best choice? If you don't know something, ask someone. Don't have pride or be ashamed to let people know you don't know. It is better to know than to make an uninformed decision. Would you rather take the wrong bus in the wrong direction, or ask the bus driver for the right bus in the right direction?

There Is No Such Thing As Security.

We go through life thinking: If I marry a man with money, he can take care of me, if I get an education, I can get a good job, if I get a job that has a union, I will have my job forever, if I cook or clean for this man, he will never leave me, if I have a baby, he will never leave me. All of these thoughts are thoughts of security. These are thoughts that people are trained to have from a childhood. We are trained from childhood to think that money, a good job and people security are supposed to make life better, but they don't.

In this life, nothing is secure. The weird thing is that most people have a false sense of security. We think all of these thoughts and they are wrong thoughts. When we are confronted with what we have believed was and is a lie, we are all broken up.

If you retrain yourself to believe what is true, you will have less heartbreak and more reality and more living your life. You will not be living from society's perspective you will be living from the truth. You know maybe I am being too rough on people, but I don't think so. We can all change it just takes some effort. I heard somewhere that it is easier to believe a lie than the truth, because the truth is just too simple for us to accept. So rethink, second guess what you hear and never fall for the lie.

Don't Let Other People Control How You Feel.

I am an American woman in my thirties and it always gets me that women let other people tell them who they are. Young women watch television shows and models and let fashion designers tell them they should look like this or should dress this way. It amazes me that they allow someone who doesn't know them tell them about themselves.

Be independent. It is okay for someone to present you with choices, but don't become a loyal subject. Subjects back in the days of kings and queens had no choices they went with whatever the ruler said. Be yourself, be different. I know being different takes courage try it you might like the results. Step out!!!!

I find that young men do the same thing. They look at all of these music stars and athletes and I say, "I want to be like him." No, you don't you want to be you. It is cool to admire someone's talents, but separate what they do from who they are.

Most young men need role models. Why not look to your father, uncle or grandfather? It doesn't have to always be a stranger.

CHAPTER 2

WOMEN

Be A Thinker

Most people don't think, especially women. Some women have great intelligence. Often they don't use it or they use it for the wrong things that make life better for them as individuals. Women usually put a lot of brain power into getting or having a man and having children. Nothing is wrong with those things, but they could think about other things.

Women don't realize that if they can out think a man, that man is not for them. Most men who are good men enjoy a thinking woman, and the men who don't enjoy the thinking, woman, forget them. Most women complain that they don't get fair treatment in the workplace. That is true. If you sit down and think about it, just out think the men who are in charge and the men in your personal life, just think for a moment about who they are. I can guarantee that, if you use your brains, you can get the end result that you are going for. If not, that person is not for your friendship or romance.

Be A Good Communicator.

This is one thing that we all have to work on. By that I mean that it may be hard, but it is necessary. Lack of communication is the one thing that causes marriages to break up. I find, even from my own experience, most people never tell you how they really feel. You can tell anybody anything as long as you know who you are dealing with and how to talk to him or her.

Communication is the key to having any good relationship. I knew a man who was not having a good life. I am a communicator. The only thing I asked him for was just to tell me what is going on and that's it. He thought I was nagging him. He didn't understand that you have to tell people what is going on they can't read your mind.

Men usually think that women want so much from them. All we want is for them just to tell us what is going on and we can work the rest out.

So please communicate well and take the time to do so.

Take Care of Your Health

Most women take better care of their health than men do. Men have an ego problem. They don't want to see a doctor until it is too late. Men say they love you, but they will die and leave you here with children to raise. Most women associate good health with good looks. Is not necessarily true that good health equals good looks. There are a lot of attractive women in very poor health. As I heard someone say: You can have a great looking house with bad plumbing. I think you should take care of your health as women, but not for vanity.

I find that most white American women have taken this too far. They are getting plastic surgery earlier and they are on all types of weight loss products, even though they are okay looking. The kicker is white American women go to the gym five days a week for two hours. I mean, come on! Taking care of yourself is one thing, but obsession is something else. Most African-American women and Latino women try to take care of their health, but they usually don't have access to good doctors. In spite of their education level or living situation, they do the best they can.

After all of that, Please take care of your health. There are all kinds of free programs to help your health needs in any part of the United States. It may not be the best, but at least it is available. Always question your doctor if you feel something that he or she says isn't right and please never be afraid to get a second opinion.

Ladies, Don't Give In To Lust Instead Of Love.

I find women will settle for a good sex life instead of real love from a good man. Don't get so hooked on a man sexually that you can't see what is really going on. Sex is suppose to be enjoyed by a husband and wife, but I am not completely deluded. We live in a world where people have sex with whomever they choose. All I am saying is, ladies, don't do it if you don't see a future with this man.

Lust is never a way to get real love. The way to get real love is to be true to yourself. By that I mean, whatever is sacred to you hold to that. Never let a man talk you out of your dreams, if he starts doing that, let him go immediately. Some people take a little time to grow but if they don't grow within a certain amount of time, keep on walking.

Real love is what you deserve. It is not just for someone else, it is for you!

Learn How To Listen To Men.

I am in my early thirties and it always amazes me how women don't listen to men. My mother taught me a lesson early in life: If you just take the time to listen to people, you will find out all about them. Most women meet men who right away start saying or acting in ways that the women don't agree with. The first thing that women say is that he will change for her. In reality, this man was saying all of these things before you took him seriously you just weren't listening or your were in denial.

I know someone who did just that. She was dating a man and he kept saying he didn't want any more children, due to the fact that he had two children: She became pregnant anyway. Who suffered the child? His father straight out rejected him. I thought, that was the woman's fault, but now that the child is here, the father should have taken responsibility. Her selfishness and her ignoring him resulted in another child growing up without a father.

I've known women who dated men and these men said they didn't want to get married. Those women paid those men no mind. Now it is five or ten years later and still no sign of marriage. I dated a man myself who told me he was going to marry me and I told him," No you are not". He said, "Yes, I am." I said that for a good reason. This was a man who wanted children and I did not. He never listened to me, but I listened to him. That saved us from making a big mistake. So, women pay attention to that man not only in words but also in actions.

Respect Your Body

Most women in this day and age have no respect for their bodies. Look at Britney Spears and even Janet Jackson. Yes, these women are beautiful and talented, but they don't have to go around showing everything. I know they have to wear clothes that are not too restrictive because of their shows, but they could be a bit more respectful of themselves and their audience.

Women today think it is okay to walk around with their pants at the crack of their behinds like Jennifer Lopez or wear a shirt with no bra and it is obvious. I told my friend one day, you will never see wealthy women with class wearing a dress bearing their midriff. She said, "You are right." I always believed you can look sexy without being trampy and showing all your business. Leave a little bit to the imagination.

Young women these days, I guess their mothers didn't teach them that their bodies don't always have to be the star of the show, or else they feel pressured by society to dress this way. Ladies, remember your body is important. It should not be open to all visitors day and night. So, ladies, respect yourselves.

Learn To Think Like A Man

I dated a man who was going through some things. Men have a black-and-white kind of thinking. They don't think in terms of hints. They only understand what is right in front of them. But that same kind of thinking can cause problems also.

I dated a man who was going through some things. We had just met when he began to neglect me and deal with his problems. He didn't realize what he was doing. I would call him and ask how things were going and he would cut me short and, tell me he was going to call me back, which he never did. So I thought to myself he probably looked at it like, "I told her I am going through things she should know." What he didn't do was look at it from my point of view, that I was only doing this as an act of human kindness. Also, he never thought that I was just concerned about him as a woman who always heard him say, "I am stressed." The end result is that we wound up not speaking at all and parting on bad terms. I was fine with it and I realized it was just his limited thinking, not mine. Also every man is not the same, some men are men of hints so you have to get that too.

The moral to the story is ladies, if you think like a man, you have less heartache in the end.

Don't Be Afraid To Get What You Need And Want!

Women live their lives for everyone else all the time, but I find that, most of the time, they live for a man.

Women will spend years in a relationship never really fulfilled, afraid that if they ask for what they want and need, they will be left alone.

Women have a real belief that a man and children make them who they are, but that belief is a lie. Always get what you need and want from a relationship, even if it costs you the relationship.

Relationships are about give and take, not just about sacrifice all the time you have to get something out of it sometime.

Women, Don't Take Men For Granted.

Men are not slaves to your will they willingly do things for you and anyone else. My grandmother never learned to drive. She thought that it was her husband's job to drive her around all the time. No, it isn't!

Men have things to do, just as women do. Women have this belief that men are just supposed to do things for them and ask no questions. Yes, a man who doesn't want to argue, but men who have any sense will check you.

Don't get me wrong, we all have duties. But when we are being overwhelmed, that is another story. Women get to the point where they don't cook for the man or dress sexy for him anymore. They look at it like, "He got me and I gave him some children so he better be grateful". Women get it together. That man will leave you for that woman who makes him feel like a man and who doesn't take him for granted.

Find Out Who You Are!

I find women go through their whole lives never really knowing who they are and they can blame no one but themselves. When you are a child you live for your parents mostly, but as you get older you are responsible for yourself. The blame game is over!

Take the time to schedule "me" days and just sit and think. Take the time to find hobbies. Hobbies bring out gifts that we never knew we had. Take the time to find out what kind of food you really like. Do you know how many people I have been around and they never knew who liked powdered donuts?

All I am saying, ladies is find out about you, because if you don't, your whole life will go by and you will never get to know the real you.

Men and Women are Into Fantasies, Not reality.

I found that most men want that fantasy of coming home to a woman who is cooking dinner, looking and smelling good, but that is not real. The sad thing is that most men really want that and, when they don't get it things can become really hairy!

For women, the fantasy is that great marriage proposal, the great wedding day and a man to take care of them financially. This is unreal also. Most women want this, but they don't marry this. Women are looking for the knight in shining armor. That is not happening.

Your best bet is to pray for the best. Most people hear about soul mates, but the fascinating thing is that most of us never meet our soul mate. We settle for whatever comes our way. That's when the problems come in. I have said that men want women who will settle. By that I mean men will get you to settle for any kind of abuse (emotional, physical and verbal) in exchange for financial security. Women will get men to settle for them by using sex, looks, children, or just good old fashioned emotional blackmail.

Both genders play games with each other in hopes of getting what they want, but it is just plain unnecessary and downright immature. If you are a mature person, you will realize that life is not about fantasy but reality and just move on from there.

Don't Look to a Man For Financial Security.

Women go through their whole lives looking for that white knight who is going to take them away from it all. Sorry, ladies, that is not happening! Men are not born to serve you. They are born to fulfill what they have been put on this earth to do. If a man gets married, he should support his wife and children, but that is not his sole purpose.

Women, do you get it that you can make just as much money as a man? Just find out what you are born to do and do it. You know, my mother always told me this and, as I got older I realized the truth in it: Women are looking for love, affection and security. Men are looking for: money, power and sex. As I got older I looked around me and said, "you know what" That is so true. A man will leave you in a relationship if you don't have sex with him and a woman will leave a man if he doesn't have something that makes her feel secure. Oprah didn't get as far as she did by depending on the man in her life. Don't get me wrong. Men have helped her along the way, but I don't think she was ever looking for that white knight.

Women, your security should be in God first but also, be secure in yourself.

The Image You Project Is The Way People Will Treat You.

Most women think, "I can wear what I want and I will still be respected for my mind." No, you won't. Even though the world has progressed, it hasn't progressed that much.

If you dress trampy or like a dumb blond, that is way you will be treated. Most women have brought into the lie: I earn my own money and my education, I should have the right to dress the way I want. Yes, I agree that you should have freedom, but there are boundaries.

When a woman gets raped, the first thing that the police will ask is, "how were you dressed?" My statements may sound cruel, but this is the world we live in and it is getting worse every day. I think that to a degree, people have too much freedom then people have no accountability for their actions. Please don't get me wrong. I am a woman and every now and then I have dressed in a certain way, but now I know better. I am a business owner, people would never take me seriously if I had the tramp look going. Ask yourself this question: Does Oprah Winfrey ever dress like a bimbo?

CHAPTER 3

MEN

Reconsider Dating Or Marrying A Man Who Is Not On Your Level.

When most women meet men, they get so hung up on the looks, sex or something else, they never stop to think: Is this man on my level? Usually the signs are there, but women ignore them. Women find out in the worst way that the men they are so crazy about is not on their level. Most women find this out when you want to do a certain thing with their lives, career wise or with their time, and they tell these men you so dearly love and the men has some kind of crazy reaction.

Then, they feel as if they have been hit in the heart with an anvil. The sad thing is that most women settle just to have a man. Don't be that woman, take your time, ask questions. As my mother told me, "If you want to know anything, just listen."

We All Should Have Priorities.

I know I have the ability to be rather rough on people sometimes. My motive is not to hurt them it is to make them think. Tough love is the best love in the long run. As I was saying, we all should have priorities, but most people are never taught that. They go through their whole lives doing the norm until someone like me comes along and says "No, that is not right." Then they get mad at me and I feel bad about standing up for my rights.

Priorities are things that need to be taught and learned. Most of us learn the hard way when we lose friends, jobs, relationships or money. All I am trying to say is if you tell people you are going to call them back, do so make them a priority. When you do call them and the person gets mad and acts as if they are bothering you. I always tell people, "You wouldn't do that to your employer, so don't do it to your children, wives, girlfriends, boyfriends, husbands or family members. We do that to all of those people because there will be no serious consequences however, if this were your job and your boss says that you have to call if you are going to be late or else, you lose your job. I'm sure you would do it.

So all I am saying is, make each person a priority! You would want to be a priority to them.

Men Want Women Who Will Settle.

Most men really want women who will settle for their lack of support. Most men are so used to women settling for their ways that, when they meet a woman who won't settle for the junk. The same man who was trying to get you winds up putting you down and calling you names. He may not say it out loud but he is definitely thinking it" Why does she want to do this or that".

I knew a man who pursued me and we became associates. He was always asking me are you going to cook for me? I told him, "I was not put on this earth to cook for you or any other man". He was used to women just saying okay to his entire request. He never thought it should be any other way. Years later, I saw this man and someone was asking why, when I attended a function, was I sitting most of the night? He responds by saying that I am stuck up! I thought to myself, "This man is upset that I wasn't stupid enough to give him the time of day so this is his revenge". By that reaction, I knew I made the right decision by not settling.

A man approached me and asked me for my phone number. I told him that dating was just not on my agenda. He just couldn't accept no. He said, "Well, everybody is busy and yada! yada! yada!" I said, "Wow! He wanted me to settle for him, a man who didn't have good grammar or dressed they way I do. I told him I was going to pre-med school (at the time) and I had my own business. Why would I settle for just being miserable? So, women, don't settle. That's what most men want, even though they wouldn't settle for your mess.

A lot Of Men Are Looking For Mothers

Men always say, "I want a woman who can cook and be there for me". That is fine and good, but women should do those things because they are good to know not because they have to do them to get a man and to keep one. Most men want these abilities in a woman because their mothers did all of that stuff for them. Many men want the same feeling of security from their childhood that their mothers provided.

As most men get older, like most women, they feel they need security and they don't want to be alone. The sad thing is that most women put up with acting like a mother to their husbands for security. When you are in a romantic relationship no one person would put up with all of a person's stuff the way a mother would. Women fall for it all the time when men say, "Are you going to cook for me?" I usually answer with, "I don't even cook for myself all the time and, better yet, "I am not your mother." Most men can't handle that they want a mother clone and they do want a clone you know. Women, don't be a mother to anyone but your children.

Never Be Afraid To Be Alone

As I've gotten older, I have found that most human beings don't like being alone. I think because being alone forces you to deal with you. I remember seeing the movie "Cast Away" starring Tom Hanks. When his character got stuck on the island, he realized he had to deal with every decision he had ever made good, bad or indifferent.

I see at a lot of women who just can't stand being without a man. Most women don't have enough courage to just say, "I'm going to take time to get to know me." Then I realized they don't want to deal with that when they can just have a man who wants the fake them. Women, take the time to be alone. You will be surprised at what you will find out about you.

Don't Marry or Date A Man Who Doesn't Listen to You or Support You.

Everyone on the planet needs some kind of support in whatever they plan to do in life. However most people don't have it and, needless to say, most people never live a lot of dreams because no one supports them. Women make that mistake all the time. They date or marry men who never support them in anything.

A woman can come to a man and say, "I want to open a business." Most men will say," why do you want to do that? I can take care of you," or "You will never succeed." To me that is both hurtful and emotionally abusive. The sad thing is most women have men in their lives like this all the time. So, women, the moral of the story is take the time to know the man.

Men Want To Remember Who They Married Or They Met, Not Who We Have Become.

I hear women and men say: Why is it that some women get a man and then let their looks go? Most women would probably disagree with me, but I have seen women do this for real. They will get a boyfriend and say, "girl I don't need to go to the gym. I've already got my man." That is the craziest thing I have ever heard.

What a lot of women don't realize is that men really do like the physical aspects of a woman and that is probably one of the reasons he was attracted to you. I am not saying that you should keep yourself up for a man you should do it for yourself.

Make Her Feel Special!

Men, do you ever hear those women you work with say, "My husband or my boyfriend is not paying me any mind, but I'm sure someone else will love to have my time." Sounds familiar, doesn't it? Women would never think about other men if that one man made her feel wanted and special.

Men have this thing that only they can do. That is, when life becomes a little too hectic, they neglect the closest thing to them whether it is girlfriend, wife or children. Everything else becomes un-important except for that thing which is causing the stress. I am not saying not to deal with your problems, but realize that your lady is important too! She needs that love and respect just the way you do. How do you feel when your wife has a baby and she is spending so much time with the baby you feel like you just don't matter any more? It's the same for her when work, friends, exercise, or social things are taking up your time.

So men, be fair! Pay attention to that woman and make her feel like she is the only one in the world for you!

If Things Are Not Great Between You, "Out of Sight, Out of Mind" sometimes Is The Best Thing.

Sometimes in a relationship things can become really strained. I find that, often the best thing to do is to spend some time apart and alone. People jump into relationships without asking questions or getting to know themselves. People have many disagreements and problems, but the best thing during this time is to stay apart. No communication, no seeing each other then you will see if you really love and miss each other and can't go on without each other.

CHAPTER 4

MONEY

There Are Three Types Of Income: Earned, Passive and Portfolio.

Most people go through their whole lives never knowing or understanding the different types of income. In my years of living, I have asked many people about money. Most of all of them have no clue. Money is your servant, not your master.

The different types of income are:

Earned – Money you work to get. Money you get for working: salary or wages.

Passive – Money you make from owning real estate, writing books, songs.

Portfolio – Money earned from investments such as stocks, bonds and savings things like that.

Most people don't know the difference they just make money and don't manage it well. So learn the difference and let it work for you.

Two companies websites and books that have helped are Richdad.com and Peakpotentials.com. It will help you become financially literate and help you along the way, if you want to be helped. Also, my mother was a financial whiz so that helped me too. My point is you can learn about money. Just research it.

Never Live Above Your Means.

This is a something I find many people do. I have watched people and myself do this. In my case I never did this for long because it is just too costly. I've seen people who will have no money, but they will look good or have a beautiful car, have no money. People do this because they are trying to impress others and are caught up in materialism.

Living above your means is a way of showing your insecurity. If you are confident in yourself, being a little strapped for a short time shouldn't make you feel bad.

People Make Enough Money. They Are Just Bad Money Managers.

Bad money management is a really bad habit. Most people make enough money, they just manage it bad. I had a girlfriend who was constantly crying, "I don't have any money." She never thought that if she stopped spending so much money on social events all the time, she would have enough to pay her bills, save and maybe invest some. Even after all of the things she went through, she still was crying about not having any money. The moral of the story is to be a better money manager. Take a class at a local college to find out how to do this. You can be financially even.

Take stock of your situation, make a budget and stick to it. Don't be afraid to get help. It may be hard at first, but you will soon see the results and they will be very good.

Never Invest Money You Can't Afford To Lose.

My mother taught me this rule as a child. If you can't afford to lose it, don't invest it. I look at stock market investors. There is always a story of someone who lost his or her life savings in the market or some crazy investment. When I see these things, I think that the broker fed into the persons greed. Why would they invest their life savings? This money is for other things.

Why would you do that to yourself? Most people's problem is they want to beat the market. You really can't do that without some working knowledge. Most people are ignorant when it comes to finances. People think to themselves, "I'm pretty smart, so I should do well," until they get burned, then they want to sue the broker and the company for bad advice. The real deal is that they should have just stayed away until they had some monopoly money.

I know you can't be protected from everything, but having extra cash just to lose is a protection.

Become A Giver!

Most people give under pressure or compulsion, not because they just love it. Actually is a way to bring in more money than you can ever imagine. Whether it is your time or your money, giving is a great thing, but most people are selfish. People give with ulterior motives.

Becoming a giver for most is hard, because most focus on themselves. This goal is easy to attain just do it! Make the decision that you are going to give until the day you leave this earth.

Money Is Your Servant

Money is meant to work for you. Most people on this planet are working for money. Once you realize that money is to work for you, life will be much better. People have this weird relationship with money, they feel that their ultimate goal in life is to work for money and not to make money work for them. The way you make money work for you is to become detached from it first of all, then study which investments you get the most pleasure from and the most financial gain from.

Investments can include being a venture capitalist which means giving someone money to start up his or her business, if the business makes a profit, you get a percentage. That is making money serve you.

CHAPTER 5
EDUCATION

Education Is Not The Big Money Ticket.

All over the world especially in America, people think that education is the big money or career ticket. It is not! I really never had a dream of going college. It was not for me personally, however I am not against it. Look at me now. I am a published author with my own publishing company, I have a cooking business and I have a garden/landscape design business. The big money ticket is your gifts, talents and what you love to do. Most people raise their children to think that going to college will make you wealthy. That is an even bigger lie!

Some of the most educated people don't earn anywhere near what people who just take a trade class. I know a young man who took a trade class. He went to school for about two years he now has a job traveling the world for what he does and makes a six figure income. I also knew another young man who drove a truck and he made a very, very good living and all he did was get a CDL drivers license. They both make more than some college professors. A long academic education is not the key for everyone. If you want to be a lawyer or a doctor, you need your education. Other than that just, be happy!

Get Education For Whatever You Plan To Do In Life.

In my last heading, I talked about education. You should get education for anything you decide to do. Even if you just take one class or read a book that is education. It doesn't have to be extreme, however lack of knowledge you will fail or make many mistakes. Don't go forth without some knowledge.

Education is something that most people without one don't value it or those with one make it their demigod. Education is a good thing, but it should be put into perspective.

Education Is A Way To Expand Your Thinking.

Education is not a ticket, it is a mind trainer. Education takes your small ideas and thoughts and expands them. If you don't have something to expand your thinking, you will be stuck in a small minded mold.

People who attend Ivy League schools know this. That is why it is hard for most who don't come from that kind of training to make it at these schools. Most people look at college as a passage, this is true but education also stretches the mind to get you to think bigger and broader.

CHAPTER 6
CAREERS

Find Out What You Love To Do.

In life, most of us don't know what we are supposed to be doing. This may sound easy to just figure out what you love. As children, we go to school, get an education, then get a job. We should learn to do what we love. You may not make a lot of money at it, at least you will be happy. When most people hear that statement, they think it is some kind of Zen like rule. No, it is true just do the research.

All my life, I was determined to do what I loved. Even if it took sixty years, I was going to live the life I loved. This can be you, too. Just do it! Don't let children, bills, etc hold you back. It may be hard but it can be done.

It may take a little time to find out what it is you love to do however, what is a little time compared to living a life of mediocrity and servitude and buying into someone else's dream?

Narrow It Down

After you have picked some careers, narrow it down. Look at the pros and cons of each. Figure out which one best suits every part of you. If you are a person who is easy going, you may want to work outdoors. In that case don't choose careers that are high pressured, such as law or medicine. If you enjoy the rush of a big crowd, maybe you should be an entertainer. Use these ideas to guide you in picking your final choice.

Take The Time To Do The Research.

Once you have realized what you love, find out if there is a way you can volunteer, read books, seminars, anything. Do any research you can on it. Watch some television shows or movies about the subject. Go to the library, spend time finding out about clubs and organizations. Then you start to see if this is truly something you love.

In my case, for my horticulture career I looked in the Yellow Pages to see if there were any horticulture schools. Once I started school, in order to get some hands on experience, I volunteered at a botanical garden. I met a woman who told me about the internship program at the garden where I was going to school. So I did the internship and graduated school. I took two gardening jobs to learn more. Then I went out and started my own business.

Every day Take Small Steps Towards That Career.

Small steps lead to the bigger goal. Do you ever watch babies who are trying to learn to walk? Every day they are crawling, pulling themselves up until one day they can stand. Then the cycle starts all over again. They know they can stand, so now it is time to do the big thing, walk. They take two steps today, then it is four steps, then, before you know it, they are full fledged walking.

Remember, every day take a step toward your bigger goal.

Visualize It and Talk About It

See yourself doing what you want in your mind's eye and eventually it will happen. Take time every day and see yourself doing these things. Then talk about it and tell one person, because if you don't talk about it you will never believe it. You don't have to tell everyone, only those who share your dreams. I hear people all the time say, "I just can't see that." That's why. With no endurance in your life, no vision, you will perish. Speak about your dreams and goals. The next thing you know they will be here.

Do it!

As Nike said "just do it"! Most people do all of the other things: Plan, think, talk but they never put any action to their words. Don't be lazy! Do everything necessary to make your dreams come true. Careers are choices. Most people don't make good choices, so please make a solid choice and make a solid plan.

Take steps every day towards your goal and, when you look back, you will be able to say, "Yes, it may have taken some time, but I never gave up.

CHAPTER 7
CHILDREN

Children Are Blessings From God And We Are Just The Caretakers.

People think that children are theirs. Yes, this is true. They are your children but they are also individuals. When people have children, they have all of these grand plans for them. They never think that the children may not want to do anything that their parents want them to do.

Children are here to grow up and affect the world, whether immediate or global. A woman said to me, "You should have children so that they can take care of you when you get old." Children should not be brought into this world with the idea in mind that they are going to take care of the parents.

When people think about having children, the motive should be just love for them and the world at large. We all were children ourselves. Somewhere along the way, we have forgotten that a parent's main job is to nurture, to help prepare children for adult life.

So, caretakers we are.

Children Have No Obligation To You, The Parent!

Children are not obligated to do anything for their parents. Children should do things because they want to and because it is the loving thing to do.

As I have gotten older, I do things for my mother just because I love her, not because my mother suffered 36 hours of labor or she cooked for me all my life. No! She is my love, my friend and my confidante.

So parents, don't think your children owe you something. They didn't ask to be brought here.

Spare The Rod And Spoil The Child!

I'm sure many of you have heard that verse of scripture before. But, do you really get it? I was brought up when parents didn't let their children rule them. It was, "Speak when you are being spoken to," and, "Be seen and not heard."

I joke all the time about how my mother had me on voice command. I did nothing when I was a child unless my mother said I could. I was not a bad child, but I used to look at all the other children who never took their parents at their word. It was a sad sight.

In this day and age parents let their small children say and do anything they want and they don't discipline them. Unbelievable! What people don't realize is that are raising a generation of spoiled people who, when they can't get their way they act up.

Imagine someone like that becoming president. Scary!

So, please discipline your children. You don't have to beat them, just let them know you are the boss. As my mother used to tell me "This is a dictatorship, not a democracy!"

Love Your Children, But Have Boundaries.

All parents would die for their children. The sad thing is some of them do. By this I mean that some parents love their children so much that they can't see who their children are and what they are doing. Children are people and that means people have the tendency to take advantage of a situation. Most parents don't know when to say that enough is enough they usually let their kids drain them dry.

My mother set boundaries for me as a child. I knew that when my mother said "No!" that was it. She had days for me and days for herself. So, as a parent and child, we had boundaries.

Raise Your Children To Be Balanced.

When children are born, they are born into a world full of things attracting their attention. Most parents don't ever think, "I don't want my children to be tossed to and fro." Parents today, I find, let everyone else raise their children but them. You can't raise your children by listening to everyone. You can take some advice, but you be the final judge Letting everyone else raise your children kind of thinking is how children turn out to be unbalanced.

You ever work with someone who's always at work, and you say to them, "You need to get a life?" That comes from the way they were raised. Their parents didn't teach them that work has its place, and so does everything else. My mother raised me to be very balanced whether I am or not that is a different story, but she did teach me balance

Parents if you raise your children to be balanced, you will have fewer worries about them when they get older.

Give Your Children A Sense Of Responsibility.

In today's world, most young people are just plain irresponsible and lazy. I really blame parents, children only do what they know. When I was growing up, my mother made me vacuum, dust, do the dishes, cook and do the laundry.

You are always going to have people who won't pull their weight, but today it is much more prevalent.

CHAPTER 8

LOVE

Love Is A Splendid Thing!

Most people go through life and never have real love. When you have never had something, you don't know how to identify it. I have seen people who have really good people in their lives and they lose them mainly because of underappreciation.

When you meet that someone, you will know it just by the first meeting it will be different from moment one. If they make you laugh when difficult times come, if they try their best to help when you don't feel like being helped, if they don't cause you any stress you feel completely comfortable around them at all times, that is real love.

Treasure it and take good care of it!

Love Is!

What is love to you? Do you know? Love is making your loved one smile just to see him smile, making them blush when you tell her that she is so beautiful or sweet.

Love is many things, but it is not abuse in any form. Love is being respectful. Love is telling the truth even though it may hurt. Love is unconditional and accepts the person for who they are.

Remember, look out for that love. It May be on the horizon at any moment!

CHAPTER 9

FRIENDS

Show Me Your Friends and I'll Show You Your Future.

For years I heard my mother say this and I didn't really know what she was trying to say. I would look at her with a blank stare. Then I grew up and it all made perfect sense.

My mother was saying that birds of a feather flock together. By that she meant that the people you call your friends can also cause your downfall. The really weird thing is, most people don't even see that their friends are leading them nowhere.

When people hear my mother and I say that, they always think we were something negative, like drugs or alcohol. No, it doesn't have to be that at all. It can be friends who don't have any dreams or desires. Those friends can be just as dangerous as drugs or alcohol.

All I am saying is, watch the company you keep!

Honesty Is Always The Best Policy.

For me, this is the best way to live. However for most people feel they can't be honest with friends, the consequences are too great. By that I mean they are afraid that their friends will stop speaking to them or that they will get mad. I found out the real motive is a fear of being alone, so they will put up with anything from friends, family or loved ones.

I was dating a man. I told him that if he would just put his cards the table, we would get along just fine. He never did that. I guess he was used to people just not saying anything and playing the hint game. Well, I have never played that game (even though they say women play this game, I don't) and I never will. He thought that me telling him to be honest was pressuring and telling him what to do. I just thought it was being real and fair. I found out that people don't want the consequences. They would just rather have the silence and think that things will go away. No, they won't, they will get worse.

I have realized that most people would rather live with a lie because it causes less friction in their minds. But, over the long haul, it will cause more problems.

So, please be honest. Even though you may risk lots of things, it is worth it.

Have Friends Who Will Support You And Celebrate You.

When I look around at most people and the friends they have, the most common thing they face is nonsupportive behavior. I have faced this. I have told people of a goal I want to reach and some of them ask "Why do I want to do that?" What for? That is not a reaction real friends are supposed to have.

Friends should support you even when the dream sounds unrealistic. Friends have no right to rob you of your dreams just because they don't have a dream of their own.

Be around people who want to see you do well and vice versa and when a goal is reached, celebrate it!

People Who Are Jealous Of You Want You Dead!

My mother heard that saying from a female pastor. The saying may sound very harsh, but it is true. When the woman began to explain what she meant, it made perfect sense. She was saying people who always oppose you and put you down, basically undermine you. They are people who just would rather see you dead in every way.

When I was a teenager, I had two friends who were jealous of me. My mother always tried to get me to see it, but, like most teenagers, I didn't. When I did realize it, I confronted my friends and ended each relationship. Those two people were jealous of my relationship with my mother and the fact that I was an only child and other things. The real deal is that they were miserable and they just wanted company. I wasn't having it!

All I am trying to say is, jealous people don't make good friends. Stay away from them!!!

See People For Who They Are, Not For Who You Want Them To Be.

I learned this at a very young age. Ninety-nine percent of people have this problem, of not seeing people for who they are. If a person has bad temper and they blow up at every little thing, someone will say, "Oh that person made them mad." Yes, maybe, but they didn't have the right to fly off the handle.

So the moral of the story is everyone has personality traits that we overlook but if you do see them accept them and make your decision.

CHAPTER 10
FAMILY

You Can't Control The Family You Were Born Into, But You Can Control The Family Circumstances.

I heard somewhere that, as spirits, we pick the families we are born into. Now I know that seems a bit much to grasp. For those who think that you can't control the family you were born into hey, you might be right. Well, in any case, you can control the family circumstances, as you get older.

You don't have to put up with alcoholic parents or drug-addicted siblings. It may hurt to leave it all behind or to love from a distance, but you may have to do this to save yourself and your dreams. If you don't, you will become a victim or have the savior syndrome, thinking that you have to save everyone from them selves. That is God's job and the person's.

So look at your family and say, "My God! If I don't change, I will die! That will cause you to change your circumstances.

Don't Let Your family Drain You.

I'm sure most people love their families, but I'm sure they sometimes wish they would go away. They don't have to go away. You just need to make a choice to not let your family drain you for every dollar you have and every ounce of your time. People don't want to admit it, but they just dislike some of their family members. The quicker you admit that, the sooner you will be free of the family drain.

Move Away!

Each family has drama. The key is, what are you going to do about it? I find that the best thing to do is move away, because you can keep your sanity and still love your family from afar.

Families are supposed to be enjoyed, not hated.

CHAPTER 11
MARRIAGE

Don't Get Married With Secrets.

I have heard my mother say this time and time again. I would always ask why someone would get married with a secret because the other person is bound to find out. I figured out why. Most of us don't want the rejection or the judgment. It is bad enough that we have to face other people's thoughts on what we do, but to have to face the one we love with something that we did is just a bit too much to take.

My mother told me a story of two people who got married. The husband in the relationship never told his new wife about his debt. She was furious when she found out about the debt he had accumulated during their dating, because now she had to help him pay off the debt. The kicker is, she didn't even create it.

My point is, put everything on the table. Even if you have to take the fury, at least you were honest.

Don't Jump Into Marriage.

Jumping into marriage is a real problem. People get married without really talking about things or going through things before marriage. My mother always told me to take my time, because it is not worth living in regret.

Marriage is not like buying a car or a new coat. It is bonding one's self legally to another person. I look at people quickly marrying, then they get upset and they want to get out. I think to myself, "If you would have taken your time maybe this would not be happening."

So take your time. Marriage is not a new car, it is your life!

Work Toward A Goal Together, Then You Will Know If You Really Want To Marry Each Other.

My mother always told me that, if a couple works toward a goal together, then they will find out if they really want to marry each other. I understood immediately. It means that, in the quest of reaching the goal, all kinds of challenges will come up and you can see how you will handle them as a couple.

People should always do this, even in the early stages of a relationship, because they will know who they are dealing with. It always amazes me when people are in relationships say, "I didn't know you knew that or why did you do that?" That is because they never took the time to look at each other and see who they are. You can do this by working toward a goal together.

Do something like plan the wedding together or decorate the house you will be living in together. You will find out then if you can take each other. Because people talk a good game until they are put into a challenging situation.

Love Your Spouse For Who They Are, Not For Who You Want Them To Be.

People get married with all kinds of expectations of each other that are unreal, when the expectations are not met they get really upset. The real deal is that they were they way they are when you married them.

I had a friend who dated a man and she always complained about his behavior. I told her that she was expecting things from him that he couldn't give her. To her it was an eye-opener, but also made her see him and herself. I have been in this same position, but I have to practice what I preach.

I always accept people for who they are but people are so used to not being accepted for who they are, that they are always playing the game or denying who they are. That makes the relationship much harder. It may take someone time to accept that they have run into someone who lets them be themselves and does not try to make them be someone else. Be patient and take the time; you will have a great marriage and relationship.

Marriage is About Compromise.

When most people get married they think that they are just supposed to always have their way. No, no. Married life is not about you, it is about us. When you get married, you have to just accept that you can't get up one day and think, "Oh I want to buy a car." No, you have to discuss this with your spouse. Even if you are rich and can easily afford it, it is just a respect factor. I think men have a problem with this more than women do because women get used to compromise early, when they have siblings, boyfriends, friends and children.

Women are taught from an early age to cook for others, clean for others, and so on. So we are always thinking of others that is why so many women get older and they don't even know who they are. They have compromised all their lives and they have come to a wall.

Don't get married with expectations. Get married with the realization that sometimes you are going to have to give up something for this person you love. If you love them, it won't be a big deal you may not like it, but to see them happy and to keep the peace, you will do it. You may not have to give it up altogether you may have to put some things on hold, but keeping the peace should be most important.

Suggested Reading

Carlson, Richard. Don't Worry, Make Money. New York: Hyperion, 1998.

Don't sweat the small stuff and it's small stuff. New York: Hyperion, 1997.

Don't sweat the small stuff with your family. New York: Hyperion, 1998.

Fisher, Mark. The Instant Millionaire: A tale of wisdom and wealth. Novato, CA: New World Library, 1990.

The Millionaire's Secrets: Life lessons in wisdom and wealth. New York: Simon and Schuster, 1996.

Kioysaki, Robert. Rich Dad, Poor Dad. New York: Warner Books, 1997.

McKee, Robert. Story: substance, structure, style and the principals of screenwriting. New York: Reagan Books, 1997.

Sher, Barbara. Live the Life you love: In ten easy step-by-step lessons. New York: Dell Publishing, 1996.

Made in the USA